ERRATA

Numbers 59, 97, 207, and 211 are deleted from the exhibition.

Number 175 duplicates 17; 197 duplicates 200.

222. **Planting Tobacco.** 1890-1900. Watercolor. Signed. 18 x 23. Lent by Mrs. Arthur E. Howlett and Mrs. Worth B. Plyler.

223. **Seated Woman: Nude.** 1890-1900. Pencil. 18¾ x 15. Lent by Mrs. Arthur E. Howlett and Mrs. Worth B. Plyler.

224. **Mountain Woman.** 1890-1900. Pencil. 15 x 11. Lent by Mrs. Arthur E. Howlett and Mrs. Worth B. Plyler.

225. **St. Anne:** Nude Study. 1902-05. Pencil. 19⅞ x 13 9/16. Lent by Mrs. Arthur E. Howlett and Mrs. Worth B. Plyler.

Elliott Daingerfield

Elliott Daingerfield

by Robert Hobbs

The Mint Museum of Art, Charlotte, North Carolina
April 14 through May 16, 1971

The North Carolina Museum of Art, Raleigh, North Carolina
May 23 through June 20, 1971

Retrospective Exhibition

PATRONS OF THE MINT MUSEUM OF ART

Staff—Mint Museum of Art

Foreword Mint Museum of Art

The Elliott Daingerfield Retrospective Exhibition makes an imperative statement about the artist's stylistic development. The Mint Museum's involvement in the creation of a retrospective for an artist of historical importance is a new direction for our exhibition program.

The idea of the exhibition germinated in a discussion at the home of Dr. Francis Robicsek in Charlotte in 1969. Dr. Robicsek owns several Daingerfield paintings, one a most impressive landscape with figures, "The Call of the Winds". In the discussion, the fact was stated that Elliott Daingerfield was probably North Carolina's most important painter and that, to date, little had been done to clarify his place of importance as an artist in the history of the 19th century painting.

This situation was a natural challenge for a museum. During my visit to Blowing Rock, N. C. to explore the possibility of arranging an exhibition of Daingerfield's work, Mrs. Worth B. Plyler and Mrs. Arthur E. Howlett, the artist's daughters, were most enthusiastic about our interest and expressed their support of the project to bring together a monumental exhibition of Elliott Daingerfield works.

Mr. Robert Hobbs, our Curator of Education, accepted the challenge of researching the artist and creating the exhibition. For the past two years Mr. Hobbs has gathered information and located paintings of significance to create a statement of Daingerfield's importance. He spent the summer of 1970 at Old Salem in a seminar of American art, conducted by Old Salem and Wake Forest University, in which he wrote and delivered a paper on Elliott Daingerfield.

The exhibition will bring together for the first time a retrospective of over two hundred works. The project has been a major undertaking for the Museum and credit should be given many people who have participated in the effort.

A special expression goes to Mrs. Arthur B. Howlett and Mrs. Worth B. Plyler for allowing us to present the exhibition of their late father's work and for being a constant source of information on the artist. The Woman's Auxiliary of the Mint Museum of Art supplied the funds to offer the exhibition to the public, as well as for publishing the catalog. Mr. Charles Stanford, Director, The North Carolina Museum of Art, has been most enthusiastic over the project and we are especially pleased that the North Carolina Museum of Art is sharing in the exhibition. We are honored that they will present the exhibition in their galleries in May and June. We would like to express appreciation to Miss Adelaide Johnston, a museum volunteer curatorial assistant, who has been very helpful to Mr. Hobbs in researching and editing the catalog. Miss Karen Colvard, a student assistant to the museum, worked many hours on cataloguing the drawings. A special expression of gratitude goes to Mr. Leon Stacks for making available research on Elliott Daingerfield.

Mr. Herbert Cohen and Mrs. Dayrell Kortheuer have given the full services of their departments to the exhibition and the results display what a real team can accomplish when a project has the enthusiasm of a dedicated staff.

Many other people were helpful in making the exhibition possible—Mrs. Barbara Lassiter, President of Reynolda House, Inc.; Dr. Cyclone Covey, Wake Forest University; Mr. Robert Vose of the Vose Galleries, Boston; Mr. Ben Williams of the North Carolina Museum of Art; Mr. Frank Manley, Miss Nina Kasanov, Miss Keating Griffiss, Professor of Art, Queens College; Miss Sue Davis, also of Queens College; Miss Mary Louise Phillips, Charlotte Public Library; and Mr. Ed Seltzer, who loaned his portrait of Daingerfield attributed to George Inness.

It is our wish that the exhibition will give new importance to the Mint Museum as a research institution and that our involvement will contribute to the quality of life in our region.

Cleve K. Scarbrough
Director

Foreword   North Carolina Museum of Art

In the past thirty-nine years after the death of Elliott Daingerfield there have been several attempts to give recognition to this North Carolina artist. In 1934 Grand Central Art Galleries of New York sponsored a memorial show for the artist and produced an excellent catalogue. Later, in 1947, the North Carolina State Art Society in Raleigh conceived an exhibit, "Daingerfield and his Contemporaries," in which works by Elliott Daingerfield were compared to those of Wyant, Weir, Blakelock, and Inness.

In 1949, Dr. and Mrs. Aubrey Lee Brooks of Greensboro donated to the State, "Evening Glow," one of Daingerfield's early works. The State Art Commission in assembling the North Carolina Museum of Art collection also recognized the importance of this painter and acquired in 1952 "The Grand Canyon," one of Daingerfield's most important works.

With the feeling that Elliott Daingerfield has made an important statement in his art concerning North Carolina and the West, the Mint Museum of Art engaged in a two-year study of the artist. This retrospective exhibition represents the culmination of this study and proves that his landscapes and religious works are indeed international in scope. The North Carolina Museum of Art is pleased to share in this exhibition which gives the public an opportunity to appreciate and study the full range of an important North Carolina artist. This comprehensive exhibition also gives the long overdue recognition to Elliott Daingerfield that he so richly deserves.

We wish to thank Mr. Cleve Scarbrough, his staff, and, in particular, Mr. Robert Hobbs, Curator of Education, for their research and work in preparation of this exhibition and catalogue.

Charles W. Stanford
Director

Elliott Daingerfield

The inhabitants of Louisville, Kentucky revered Blind Jenny's prophecies in much the same manner as the ancient Greeks had followed the oracles at Delphi. Although she was born a slave, Blind Jenny was compensated by the gift of second sight. One can imagine the old sage slowly rocking on a chair cushioned with remnants of worn carpeting, mumbling fortunes in her home-spun jargon. One Louisville resident, Anna Grainger, came to Blind Jenny to hear what events the future would bring. Blind Jenny decreed, "You will marry an artist who will become famous for painting two places. One will be a huge rock in the South and the other a big red hole in the West." Little did Anna Grainger realize that Blind Jenny's prophesy referred to Elliott Daingerfield, an artist whose acquaintance she would make during the following summer when she traveled to a small village in North Carolina near the ordained rock, Blowing Rock.[1]

The year was 1894. For the past eight summers Elliott Daingerfield had been known as a regular habitué in Blowing Rock where he had originally come to recuperate from an illness. When he first sighted Anna Grainger at a hotel in Blowing Rock, he knew he would marry this girl. Anna Grainger had very much the Madonna-type face which Elliott had been painting before he had even met her. As he gazed at her, he saw one of his paintings incarnated. Many years later when asked by his daughter if it were a physical attraction which brought him to Anna Grainger, he replied, "Physical attraction, nothing! It was one spirit recognizing another and knowing it instantly."[2]

An anecdote such as this is only a beginning.

Elliott Daingerfield was born in Harpers Ferry, Virginia,[3] on March 26, 1859, the same year as John Brown's famous raid. Daingerfield, however, soon became a citizen of North Carolina (in 1861) when his father, Captain John Elliott Parker Daingerfield, received an order from General Robert E. Lee to command the Arsenal at Fayetteville. Growing up in the South during the Civil War and the Reconstruction period would certainly leave an indelible impression on any child. To one with the sensitivities of young Elliott it endowed him with an intense desire to succeed and to shake off the well worn cloak of shabby gentility so carefully cultivated by most southerners.

While he was living in Fayetteville, Daingerfield had already started to paint. According to an existing story, Elliott's older brother, Archie, gave

[1]Interview with Marjorie Howlett and Gwendoline Plyler, "Westglow," Blowing Rock, North Carolina, 19 October 1970.

[2]Tape of Interview with Marjorie Howlett and Gwendoline Plyler by Joseph Dulaney, "Westglow," Blowing Rock, North Carolina, 4 September 1967.

[3]Harpers Ferry, Virginia became Harpers Ferry, West Virginia June 20, 1863.

Monk Smelling a Bottle of Wine
1880. Oil. 20 x 13
Mrs. Worth B. Plyler

1

him a box of watercolors for Christmas, and Elliott, picking up the water-colors, began to paint exquisite paintings.[4] There remains a certain element of truth in this story as many of his early watercolors demonstrate the same quality which he sustained throughout his life. During this youthful period, Daingerfield studied with Mrs. William McKay, a local china painter. Later, Daingerfield apprenticed himself to a local photographer from whom he learned to take pictures and carefully tint the results.

Nevertheless, Fayetteville, North Carolina in 1879 did not provide the stimulus which Elliott Daingerfield needed to become a painter. It is unlikely that any place in the South during those years after the Civil War could provide the proper incentive for a man of his calibre. Where could he find the coterie of America's finest painters, and where would the competition be great and the chances of success slim? Where else but in New York City.

At first Daingerfield tried to compromise by studying in Norfolk, Virginia, where he worked with an unknown artist for six months. But the urge to go to New York loomed greatly in his mind, and Elliott Daingerfield at the age of twenty-one with only a few dollars in his pocket set out for the great city. North Carolina, however, would always be his home: he had attachments there—family, friends, and the mountains. He would come back to summer in North Carolina beginning in the year 1885 and would build three of his homes in Blowing Rock.

For the present his development as a painter depended upon the training, competition, and frenzied world of New York. It seems Elliott Daingerfield had to get away from his southern environment in order to view it more clearly. With a little perspective he could distill his impressions into a coherent pictorial form. And New York in the 1880's would serve as a perfect backdrop for understanding the tranquil world of the North Carolina mountaineer and the mountains themselves.

On his arrival in New York, Elliott Daingerfield suffered the usual deprivations which many young artists assume when their technique and maturity cannot keep pace with their ambitions. Numerous stories related by the artist's daughters describe their father's looking for jobs unsuitable to his temperament such as painting lampshades and Christmas cards.[5] Fortunately for Daingerfield this period of drifting ended quickly. He had lived in New York less than a month when he made the acquaintance of Walter Satterlee, an associate member of the National Academy of Design, whose talent at illustration can be compared to that of Norman Rockwell. Daingerfield became Satterlee's studio boy. Early each morning he started work by cleaning the studio, laying out the paints, stretching canvases and setting up still life arrangements for the students who studied with Satterlee. In return for his labors he was allowed to paint until nine o'clock each morning at which time Satterlee would come into the studio and criticize his work. The arrangement was pleasing to both Elliott and Satterlee, and soon he was

[4]Margaret McMahan, "State's Most Noted Painter Had Close Ties with City," *Fayetteville Observer,* 10 October 1965, Section D, p. 1.

[5]Interview with Gwendoline Plyler, Monroe, North Carolina, 10 February 1971.

The Harvest
1892. Oil. 19½ x 15½
Mr. E. N. Seltzer

engaged as an instructor in Satterlee's still life class where he taught for four years. During this period Daingerfield also studied intermittently at the Art Students' League.

Even during his first year in New York Daingerfield exhibited in the National Academy of Design, his first entry being "The Monk Smelling a Bottle of Wine" (Plate 1). One can easily understand why an artist would want his work to be accepted by this institution. The National Academy of Design represented the official arbiter of art. Whoever exhibited in its shows was worthy of attention, and a member's work seemed as sound an investment for a collector as a blue chip stock.

With the acceptance of his pictures by the academy to his credit Daingerfield abandoned Satterlee's tutelage. The year 1884 became a decisive one for him as me met George Inness for the first time. Although he never studied with Inness formally, Daingerfield became a close friend and gleaned certain elements from the Inness style.

In 1891 he moved into the Holbein Studios of West Fifty-fifth Street. J. Scott Hartley, son-in-law of George Inness and one of the leading sculptors of his era, had built the studios over a group of stables in the early 1870's in an effort to provide a place for American artists to work. Almost all of the important artists of the late Nineteenth Century managed to be tenants at the Holbein. J. Alden Weir, George Inness, Homer Martin, Childe Hassam, George de Forest Brush, John Singer Sargent, Frank Duveneck, Winslow Homer, and W. H. Wyant worked at the Holbein Studios at some point in their careers.[6]

In the 1870's when American artists were struggling against European competition, there were no dealers' galleries on Fifth Avenue in which they could hold one man shows or otherwise exploit their work. They found a means out of this difficulty by having "co-operative studio teas" and "at homes." On certain days receptions were given; every artist sent cards to friends and persons interested in art. All doors were thrown open so that visitors could wander through the studios. In this way many pictures were sold and reputations made at the Holbein.

It was an element of good fortune for Daingerfield to form an association with the Holbein. Here he worked in a studio near George Inness and became a colleague of the old master of American landscape painting. From Inness, he learned to glaze his canvases by applying layers of colors over other layers of colors and inserting thin coats of varnish between them. George Inness, enjoying the opportunity to promote a young artist, acquired several Daingerfields himself. Often he would send his collectors to buy paintings by the young North Carolinian artist with the quip: "Why pay such exhorbitant prices for my paintings when you can acquire works by this young artist for a fraction of the cost?"[7]

[6]Lula Merrick, "Holbein Studios, First in City, Are to Go, But Memories Will Be Bright," *The Sun and New York Herald*, 7 March 1920, p. 7.

[7]Howlett and Plyler, Interview, 19 October 1970.

Mysterious Night
1895. Watercolor. 25 x 20
Mrs. Arthur E. Howlett and
Mrs. Worth B. Plyler

3

15

The Story of the Madonna
c. 1900. Oil. 44½ x 34½
Mr. Charles A. Cannon

16

St. Elizabeth: Drapery study for
"The Magnificat" in The Lady Chapel
of The Church of St. Mary The
Virgin, New York City.
1902-06. Pencil. 20 x 12 9/16
Mrs. Arthur E. Howlett and
Mrs. Worth B. Plyler

7

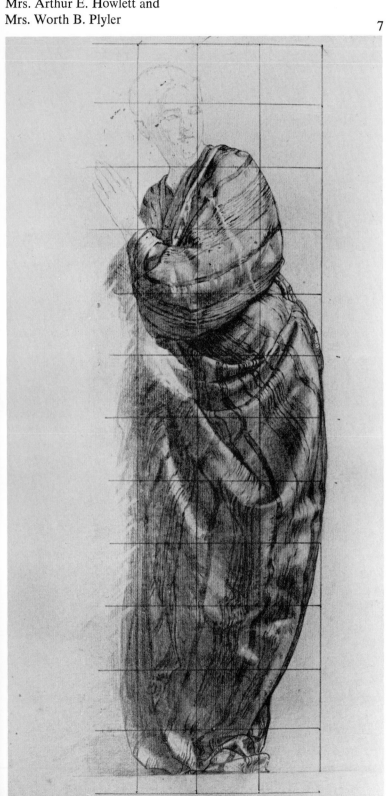

Elliott Daingerfield's paintings during this period reflect his childhood in North Carolina. The subjects usually describe simple farmers employed in everyday occupations. "The Harvest" (Plate 2) exemplifies this style of painting. Dated 1892 and dedicated to J. William Fosdick, a friend of the artist, this canvas contains a young woman holding large bundles of hay under each arm. The rugged strength of figures like this led critics to apply the appellation American Millet to Daingerfield. The subject of this painting does remind one of Millet with its lack of condescension toward the young woman. One feels that this woman symbolizes the stability which the United States achieved after the Civil War. In each arm she carries a bundle of hay suggesting the harvest as the compatibility of the North and the South. By placing the conflagration in the background, the artist signifies the end of the war.

Daingerfield may have thought of his works during this period when he wrote:

> . . . the minds of men fatigued in the hourly struggle for wealth and its keeping, seeking relief from the prosaic, ready to be led into the rich paths of romance what is it we lack? What then but the interpreter the man will find beneath or within it all the spirit of life? The morgue, the gutter, and the slum are not significant of a people who are at once clean, wholesome, and optimistic. These three words may well be a text for us. That we may think cleanly, paint wholesomely, with an optimism born of faith in a people who are the engrafted strength of many; and for a creed, that principle which is the first and last letter of Art—the principle of Beauty.[8]

Many artists of the late Nineteenth Century idealized their subjects by employing figures of women as allegories to symbolize concepts such as chastity, culture, war, and the Western mind. The allegory which often appears obvious is unpalatable to the Twentieth Century aesthetic. In "The Harvest" the significance of the woman does not intrude itself on the spectator since the painting can be understood as merely a figure of a woman carrying two bundles of hay.

The paint quality witnessed in this canvas contains seeds of Daingerfield's mature style of painting. Already the colors glow with a richness attained by successive layers of glazing. In order to destroy the dead surface and give resonance to his work the artist evolved a system of alternating layers of opaque and transparent colors and carefully balancing the warm and cool tones. Although he delicately blended many of the strokes, Daingerfield could not resist the temptation of dashing a few strokes over the surface to give the painting a little more spontaniety. As the eye jumps from one of these accents of brushstrokes to another, the figure, the fire, and the sky move in a flux.

At the same time that the critics labeled him the American Millet, Daingerfield discovered a comrade spirit in Algernon Blackwood, a contem-

[8]Elliott Daingerfield, "Nature Versus Art," *Scribner's Magazine*, XLIX (February, 1911): 253-56.

Prophet: Drapery Study for the
"Epiphany" in The Lady Chapel of
The Church of St. Mary The
Virgin. New York City.
1902-05. Pencil. 17 5/16 x 15 13/16
Mrs. Arthur E. Howlett and
Mrs. Worth B. Plyler

8

porary writer with an intense pre-occupation for the psychic. Often Blackwood's descriptions relate so closely to Daingerfield's paintings that one marvels the two men never met.[9] His "Mysterious Night" (Plate 3), exhibited at the New York Water Color Club Exhibition in 1895, invites comparison with a paragraph from Blackwood's story "The Willows".

> I gazed across the waste of wild waters; I watched the whispering willows; I heard the ceaseless beating of the tireless wind; and, one and all, each in its own way, stirred in me this sensation of a strange distress. But the willows especially: forever they went on chattering and talking themselves, laughing a little, shrilly crying out, sometimes sighing—but what it was they made so much to do about belonged to the secret life of the great plain they inhabited. And it was utterly alien to the world I knew, or to that of the wild yet kindly elements. They made me think of a host of beings from another plane of life, another evolution altogether, perhaps, all discussing a mystery known only to themselves. I watched them moving busily together, oddly shaking their big bushy heads, twirling their myriad leaves even when there was no wind. They moved of their own will as though alive, and they touched by some incalculable method, my own keen sense of the horrible.

The two men are pantheists. For them Nature is composed of spirits; it contains a mysterious quality which both repels and excites the onlooker. Algernon Blackwood felt only one craving: to get away to the wild abandon of nature. In Daingerfield's watercolor one is drawn into the landscape immediately. The dark and omnious foreground gives way to a background bathed in moonlight which compels the viewer to venture forth into the landscape unaware that the enticing light will retreat a little further, only to leave him stranded in the same untamed forces of nature as Blackwood described.

Sometimes an artist's criticism of his contemporaries' work provides an excellent clue to the understanding of his own work. This is the case with Elliott Daingerfield. In an article on John Singer Sargent for the *New York Herald*, Daingerfield explains the way he prefers to handle watercolor:

> In the method I am speaking of, the paper being sopping wet, the colors sometimes are sponged in and out. And just as painters in oil will use cuttlefish bone to rub down parts of the painted surface in order to obtain desired effects, so in the watercolor work of the Dutch and French the artist does not hesitate to use sandpaper. He is working for quality. Whether he paints in wash, uses opaque color or even works entirely in gouache is a matter of indifference to him, so long as he achieves the effect he is after. With white paper the Dutchman, as his paper begins to dry, lifts out the color

[9]Several years after her father's death Marjorie Howlett made a voyage to Europe. While she was visiting in England, she met Algernon Blackwood who, to her surprise, was familiar with Daingerfield's paintings and for a long time had regarded this American artist as a comrade spirit. Interview with Marjorie Howlett, Hotel des Artistes, New York, New York, 6 January 1971.

Slumbering Fog
c. 1905. Oil. 29⅞ x 35⅞
The Metropolitan Museum of Art

9

here and there with a sponge, the result being that the white of the paper comes through with great brilliancy.[10]

A close examination of "Mysterious Night" demonstrates that watercolor is not used in the traditional manner. Daingerfield does not respect the surface of the paper as the English aquarellists do. By sanding the paper he provides a textured surface on which to lay washes. This rough texture allows the colors to sink into the paper so as to become part of it and endows the painting with the characteristics of a pastel. The inner glow of the moonlight results from the application of yellow tones which are partially sponged out before the watercolor dries on the paper. After the entire surface is painted in this wet fashion, Daingerfield uses a dry brush to put in small accents as the fence and the branches on the tree.

While he was culminating his early style of painting in the last decade of the Nineteenth Century, another style and subject matter began to attract his attention. Within a year after his marriage to Anna Grainger, Elliott Daingerfield distinguished himself by a religious painting, "Madonna and Child". Several years earlier he had explored religious subjects, but never before had his attempts been met with such acclaim. A Cincinnati newspaper in 1896 pronounced him ". . . as having a path apart from the common highways of artists."[11] The painting, acquired by Haley Fiske, President of Metropolitan Life Insurance Company, was reproduced on the December, 1896 cover of *The Churchman*. The "Madonna and Child" enjoyed great prestige: copies of it were made and sold throughout the United States to those who wished to have a reproduction of a religious painting in their home.[12]

Why did this painting and others like it as "The Child of Mary", "The Holy Family", and "The Story of the Madonna", (Plate 4) for which he won the Clarke Prize in 1902, became so popular? Of course, the uniqueness of such subject matter for an American artist might serve as a reason for its recognition. Feeling an inclination towards American religious painting was being innovated by Daingerfield, many critics hailed his "Madonna and Child" as the American Madonna.

The path of acceptance for religious art had already been paved in England by the Pre-Raphaelite Brotherhood in the 1840's. Wishing to revolt against the fashionable painting of the time in which trivial, sentimental subjects were treated within an accepted range of coloring and lit accordingly to the rules of academic chiaroscuro, the Pre-Raphaelites, headed by William

[10]In this article Daingerfield's attitudes toward the handling of watercolor are quoted. Gustave Kobbe, "Mr. Sargent's Latest Pictures," *The New York Herald*, Magazine Section, 5 November 1918, p. 5.

[11]This quotation is taken from a newsclipping in Elliott Daingerfield's scrapbook. For many of these newsclippings information such as date and name of the newspaper or magazine was deleted.

[12]The painting was published and copyrighted in 1896 by James Pott and Co., of Fourth Avenue and 22nd Street. Also, Woodbury E. Hunt, an art published in Concord, New Hampshire, offered prints of this painting to his customers.

Christ Stilling the Tempest
1905-10. Oil. 20 x 24
The Metropolitan Museum of Art

Holman Hunt, John Everett Millais, and Dante Gabriel Rosetti, aimed at expressing genuine ideals. They studied directly from nature and envisioned events as they must have happened rather than as the rules of design required. Although he painted later than the Pre-Raphaelites, Daingerfield shared with them an idealistic purpose: the sincere desire to inspire his public by faithfully illustrating the Gospels. According to his daughters, Daingerfield hung in his studio a large crucifix from Salisbury Cathedral.[13] Before he began to paint, this artist would kneel in front of the cross in prayer. He expressed in these prayers the desire to produce pictures which would inspire the highest good. Such an attitude acknowledges his similarity to that of the Pre-Raphaelites.

Daingerfield's contemporaries must have felt that his religious painting stemmed from a sincerity of purpose. A contemporary description of the artist explains that what one experiences in his work is revealed in his personality:

> He is an atmospheric looking man, a good deal like his pictures. His expression is poetic and he has large imaginative eyes. Art is two-sided, and the subtle persuasion that makes his pictures an inspiration, seems to be reflected in his voice. His tones are as softly modulated as those of a sweet singer.[14]

At the beginning of each year human beings tend to take stock of the former year, sweep clean the debris, and begin anew with a clean slate. Surely with the advent of a new century this human tendency must be greatly amplified. For Daingerfield the beginning of the Twentieth Century meant changes in his style of painting. Gone was the Nineteenth Century and with it the tender and sentimental Victorian attitudes which found expression in his American Millet paintings. The new century called for a grander and more universal theme, and the religious paintings which he had already begun in the last years of the Nineteenth Century were to serve as his mode of expression during the first years of the Twentieth Century.

Even these religious paintings appear more grandiose in the Twentieth Century. In 1902 he was commissioned by Haley Fiske to paint a series of large murals for the Lady Chapel in St. Mary the Virgin in New York City.[15] It was the commission of the decade, and Elliott Daingerfield suddenly the man of the moment, inspired a large audience of admirers. "The Epiphany," the first of these murals, which was completed by 1905, depicts the Adoration of the Magi. The second mural, "The Magnificat", was finished a year later. In this the artist chose to portray the Virgin after the annunciation when She sings a hymn of thanksgiving. To the right of the Virgin, he represents the Apostolic College of Saints who are especially im-

[13]Howlett and Plyler, Interview, 19 October 1970.

[14]This is taken from an 1896 newsclipping found in the artist's scrapbook.

[15]St. Mary the Virgin, built in 1895, was one of the first churches in the United States to use dramatic lighting i.e. spotlights and recessed lights.

Autumn
1907. Oil. 30 x 36
Mrs. Worth B. Plyler

High Noon
1908. Oil. 48 x 36
Mrs. Arthur E. Howlett and
Mrs. Worth B. Plyler

28

Sky Study for "High Noon"
1907-08. Oil on cardboard.
7¾ x 5½
Mr. and Mrs. David H. Rankin   13

Windswept
Before 1917. Oil on cardboard. 5 x 5¾
Miss Mandy Richardson

Archangel Michael: Nude study
for "The Magnificat" in The
Lady Chapel of the Church of
St. Mary the Virgin, New York City.
1902-06. Pencil. 19⅜ x 11 3/16
Mrs. Arthur E. Howlett and
Mrs. Worth B. Plyler

5

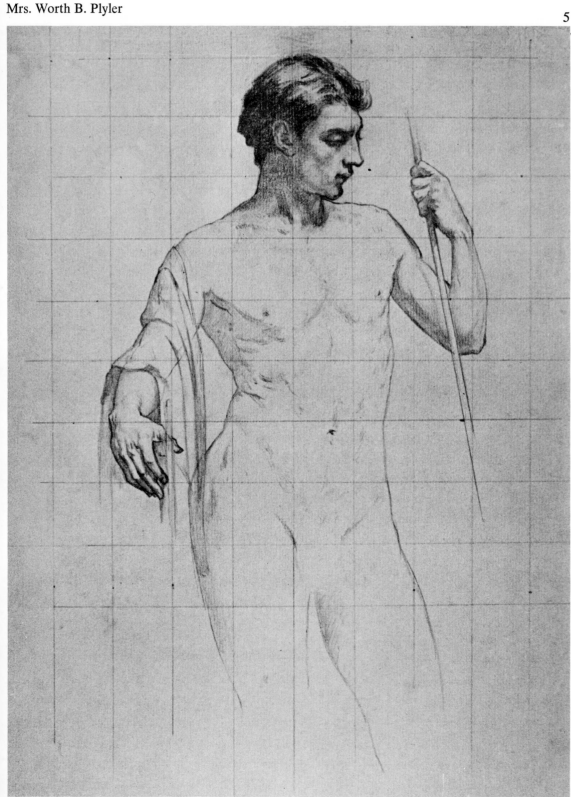

Archangel Michael: Armour and Drapery
study for "The Magnificat" in the
Lady Chapel of The Church of St. Mary
The Virgin, New York City
1902-06. Pencil. 19⅞ x 15 13/16
Mrs. Arthur E. Howlett and
Mrs. Worth B. Plyler

18

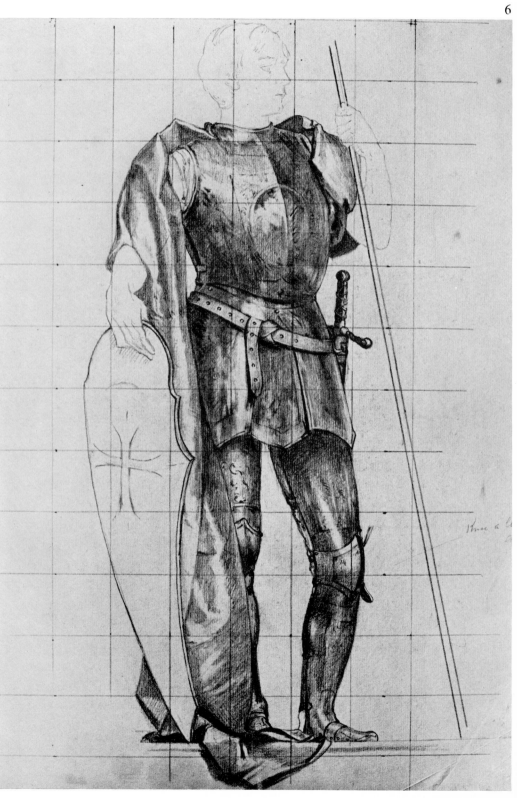

The Grape Arbor
1900-17. Oil on cardboard. 7½ x 9
Miss Patricia Carnell

portant to the Virgin. For many of the figures Daingerfield made portraits of his acquaintances and even included himself in the role of the cardinal who stands second from the right in the mural.

An astonishingly large number of the drawings for these murals have been preserved by the artist's daughters. Close scrutiny of these pencil studies reveals Daingerfield's precise draughtsmanship and painstakingly careful attention to details before the murals were painted. As in the academic tradition the figures are conceived in a series: they are first drawn nude and then clothed. The drawings of Archangel Michael (Plates 5 and 6) nude and then in armour serve as a good example of this. Around the figure of Archangel Michael, the grid system establishes the scale which Daingerfield magnifies on the large mural. The artist tends to view the subjects in a plastic manner and depends upon light and shadow more than definite lines to give his drawings character. The magnificent drapery study for Saint Elizabeth (Plate 7) testifies to this fact; the quality of the highlights and shadows suggests the sheen of heavy silk. Also, in the figure of the prophet (Plate 8) one picks out specific contours with difficulty. The quality of the light and shadow establishes the thoughtful mood of the prophet, and definite accents are relegated to a minor position. Daingerfield tends to present his forms in a more linear manner, however, in the finished murals.

In an article on "Color and Form"—Their Relationship" Elliott Daingerfield defends the position that a colorist as himself is not of necessity barred from the ability to draw:

> It is said, too, that great colorists never draw well. Perhaps, this is true, I do not know—Turner seems to have drawn very well at times—but there is nothing in color itself to prevent one drawing well.[16]

In spite of his defense that an artist can be both an excellent draughtsman and a colorist, Daingerfield chose to emphasize color in all of his work after 1906. The paintings reflect a feeling for color coupled with a physical reaction to paint, strong, rich, and oily, varying in thickness from the consistancy of butter to the consistency of milk. Often the sensation of color affects an artist in a powerful way because he can involve himself with color to such an extent that he becomes a color inebriate and loses nearly all sense of form.[17] For this reason Daingerfield tempers his color with a full range of grays as

> "Color however rich, is dependent upon gray, for gray makes possible gradation, and gradation is the means by which the flat surface of canvas or panel is translated into the near and far of form."[18]

[16]Daingerfield "Color and Form—Tneir Relationship," *The Art World*, III (December, 1917), 179-180.

[17]Ibid.

[18]Ibid.

Sketch of The Red Sofa Cushion
1915-20. Oil on cardboard. 10 x 12
Mr. E. N. Seltzer

Daingerfield also asserts that he is not ready to return to the barbaric excitement of a spot of yellow or red because he cannot give up the exquisite delicacy of nature with her sumptuousness of color and the magic of her grays.[19]

The painting, "Slumbering Fog," (Plate 9) beautifully demonstrates how a full range of gray tones achieves a coloristic effect. The real subject of the canvas becomes the fog which spreads over the entire surface dimming the effect of the sun and producing a gray haze. Daingerfield builds up the foreground with dark grays which fade into happier grays tinged with yellow in the middle ground. The background recedes as the warm grays go into cooler tones. A very calming effect is conveyed by this symphony of grays.

In a painting such as "Christ Stilling the Tempest" (Plate 10) Daingerfield reveals how the chameleon-like grays have a magic carrying power which holds together a combination of rich colors. The fury of the painting immediately excites an observer. All is rendered in a state of terrific movement much like the fury of Albert Pinkham Ryder's paintings. The colors, mostly greens, reds, and blues with splashes of light mauves, are applied in long, lean strokes each catapulting over the other; and the different colors give the surging composition an unbelievable richness. What saves the painting from becoming crude is that most of the colors are of the same tonal value with the dark and light grays enhancing the contrast. In paintings like this Daingerfield thinks in terms of colors which are mostly of the same value.

Several paintings of the first decade of the Twentieth Century with their light glowing color attest to Elliott Daingerfield's personal happiness. Some of these were painted purely for pleasure. "Autumn," (Plate 11) completed in 1907, expresses thanksgiving for the bountiful harvest which Daingerfield suggests in the foreground by the grand display of fruits and vegetables. The real harvest, however, is the artist's two young daughters Marjorie and Gwendoline. His wife fulfills the theme of the harvest by acting as Ceres, the Roman goddess of agriculture. An oil sketch[20] indicates that the idea for this painting was conceived several years earlier, before the birth of his younger child. Perhaps the incentive to complete "Autumn" came from the joy Daingerfield experienced in having two daughters for he gave the finished painting to Gwendoline when she was four. A marvelous story relates that Kaiser Wilhelm of Prussia wanted this canvas and even sent an emissary to the United States to acquire it at any cost. The Kaiser's messenger was daunted when Daingerfield told him that "Autumn" belonged to his daughter. It would be her decision to sell the painting. Much to the chagrin of the Kaiser and the emissary, the offer was refused.[21]

[19]Ibid.

[20]This oil sketch from the Charles A. Cannon collection is included in the exhibition.

[21]Howlett and Plyler, Interview, 19 October 1970.

Moonlight
1910-20. Oil. 31 x 36
Hirschl & Adler Galleries

Another painting "High Noon", which was completed in 1908, (Plate 12) exhibits this same joy. Anna Grainger Daingerfield is shown taking a stroll with the two young children at the Windwood garden near Blowing Rock. Light permeates everything, and the canvas becomes more impressionistic than any other work by the artist. The flowers on the left are patches of pure color while the shadows on Mrs. Daingerfield's shawl and dress become a glorious blue green. Rather than employing the short, choppy strokes of the Impressionists, Daingerfield uses a longer stroke typical of his later work.

A scintillating sketch (Plate 13) for this work exists and makes an excellent comparison to the finished painting. The sketch, a small oil study on cardboard, reveals large trumpet-shaped clouds which Daingerfield painted in only a few moments. The clouds, conceived in thick, heavy paint, spiral richly through the sky. With a few strokes of the brush in the foreground Daingerfield creates miles of mountains and trees. Cloud studies of this type invite comparison with those of old masters like Constable who made many cloud studies that noted the wind direction, type of cloud, and time of year. In the finished painting Daingerfield employs the basic format of the sketch with the sky still occupying the majority of the picture; however, the clouds are controlled so as not to compete with the center of interest, the figures in the foreground. The mountains, which are powerful in the sketch, fade into a light blue haze in the completed picture.

The superior quality of oil sketches such as the cloud study for "High Noon" can alone affirm Elliott Daingerfield's importance as an artist. From these studies one can sense the way in which the artist initially reveals himself on canvas. These studies are done on a small format in which each brush stroke discloses a specific movement of the artist's hand. Because he can follow the artist's train of thought, the observer feels on close terms with him. At first the sky and clouds are attacked with brushes loaded with paint, then the mountains are defined, and the trees and other details become distinct by scratching through the paint with the blunt end of the brush. If a mistake is made, a rag can wipe it away in seconds, and only a few moments are invested in the painting. A sketch serves as a good way for the artist to limber up. Just as a pianist plays chords before working on a piece of music, an artist like Daingerfield may spend thirty minutes sketching in oils. But the sketch remains, whereas the chords or improvisations, result in a piece of music well played or a variation on a theme. With both there appears an element of play. In order to loosen up, Daingerfield might have taken out his brushes to see how quickly he could size up a landscape, without worrying about technique since he just wanted the summation of an idea. At other times sketching could be used to register quickly an impression. Because many of these sketches result from an immediate impulse, the artist often has no time to consider each gesture or to notice what he says about himself. He will have time for that later when he reviews his work and decides to refine, distill, and calculate on the immediate response.

In 1917 Daingerfield wrapped in a packet many of the oil sketches

Apple Blossoms
1890-1910. Oil. 15½ x 19½
Miss Mandy Richardson

18

38

which he had painted since the beginning of the century; he wrote on the outside of the brown wrapping paper his name and the date. It seems almost as if Daingerfield had to wrap up these sketches and conceal them in a secret place (not to be found until 1969)[22] because they exposed too much of himself. If he allowed these sketches to be shown, it would be the same as appearing undressed in public. He could show his finished landscapes because he had time to consider what went into these paintings; the small sketches, however, are fantastic bursts of spontaniety revealing his innermost self.

Most of the sketches in this exhibition came from the packet which Daingerfield had hidden away in 1917. A discussion of a few will suggest qualities which all of them have in common. "Blowing Rock, 1905"[23] exemplifies Daingerfield's immediate reaction to paint. Beginning not with sharp drawing but with vague masses of color that he gradually refines, he expertly creates shapes which imply the elements they contain. The strokes of paint glow with an unbelievable opulence. The forms assume realistic shapes only when he regards the composition at a distance. Looking closer the small sketch seems to be reminiscent of abstract expressionism. Although Daingerfield completed this study in a few moments, he proves his genius by employing fluid brushstrokes to pull together broad areas of color. "Windswept" (Plate 14) another small sketch, is built around only one idea—the furious movement of the wind over the trees and the clouds. But what an idea! The trees, only suggested, begin to move in the same wavelike motion as the clouds. In the clouds Daingerfield culminates this action with large blobs of white paint which resemble the spray from a terrific wave of water. The flickering of sunlight on a grape arbor at Daingerfield's home Wind wood becomes the theme for another sketch, "Grape Arbor" (Plate 15). Small dashes of brush strokes dance about the panel as the sunlight disappears into shade under the vines and emerges in another portion of the sketch. One is amazed to view the subtle nuances of tone and colors in this exercise. Always the colors are kept on a low key but display great richness and variance.

Often, Daingerfield's landscapes stem from his imagination and do not represent a particular locale. Daingerfield once declared, "if one must paint from nature, paint from it meaning away from it."[24] In his analysis of George Inness, Daingerfield wrote, "The greatest of his pictures were painted out of what people fondly call his imagination, his memory—painted

[22]Daingerfield placed this packet of oil sketches behind a shelf of books in his library at his summer home, "Westglow" in Blowing Rock, North Carolina. The sketches were discovered by his daughters in the summer of 1969.

[23]This sketch from the collection of Mr. and Mrs. William G. Shelton is included in the exhibition.

[24]The actual quotation made by Daingerfield in "Nature Versus Art," p. 255 is:
The oft-repeated phrase, "Paint from Nature," is a good one if properly understood: Paint from—in the sense of away—not by her, lest she has her way with you and not you with her. My meaning is made clear by quoting from one of our very distinguished artists—"What we want is less nature and more art."

Genius of The Canyon
1913. Oil. 35 x 47
Mrs. Arthur E. Howlett and
Mrs. Worth B. Plyler

19

within the four walls of a room, away from and without reference to any particular nature; for he himself was nature."[25] To these landscapes Daingerfield applies the term "synthetic."[26] By "synthetic" he refers to the synthesis of color, brushwork, and composition working together to provide in the viewer's mind a more perfect truth than one might find in nature alone.

The sketch, "The Red Sofa Cushion" (Plate 16), which was painted about 1917, exemplifies Daingerfield's handling of a synthetic landscape. According to the artist's oldest daughter, when he envisioned this sketch of a blazing sunset, he gazed at the reflection of a red cushion on a mahogany sofa. The design of the wood seemed to make a weird, wonderful sort of tree. Where the high polish of the mahogany shone out, emerged a glint of water, and the reflection of the red cushion into the mahogany appeared like a great, angry setting sun in the landscape.[27]

Daingerfield's idea of the synthetic landscape denotes more than a clever mind capable of producing a landscape from the imagination. A painting must not merely imitate the model as the subject does not endow a picture with importance. A subject becomes memorable only if the artist can utilize it to express ". . . some profound love or belief."[28] And the love or belief expressed by Daingerfield in his landscapes remains a type of pantheism, a spiritual attitude toward nature. The vitality and beauty of nature emerge as themes because the aliveness manifests the working of the spirit of God and the beauty represents God's work.

At an 1895 alumnae lecture for the Girls High School in Louisville, Kentucky, Daingerfield announced his definition of art:

> "Art is the principle flowing out of God through certain men and women, by which they perceive and understand the beautiful. Sculpture, architecture, pictures, and music are the languages of the spirit."[29]

Thus, for Daingerfield, it would have been impossible to paint without being conscious of God. Both the landscapes and biblical paintings spring from the same source and in different ways make an effort to disclose "the beautiful."

[25]Daingerfield, "George Inness," *Century*, XCV (November, 1917), 71.

[26]Daingerfield, "J. Francis Murphy—Painter," *Scribner's Magazine* LXI (February, 1917), 127-30. In this article Daingerfield states:
> As time has passed, Mr. Murphy has become, as most thoughful artists do, more and more synthetic. His pictures are broader, less worked out in detail, but big and calm, the envelope of an atmosphere beautifully adjusted.

[27]Howlett and Plyler, Interview by Joseph Dulaney, 4 September 1967.

[28]Daingerfield, *Ralph Albert Blakelock* (New York: Privately Published by F. F. Sherman, 1914), p. 10. The complete statement is:
> A work of art should express some profound love or belief in the heart of the artist—belief in the harmony, in the design, in the effect, as well, as in the meaning, else it is merely a work of craft,—handicraft,—and to be valued as such.

[29]*Louisville Courier Journal*, 19 April 1895.

The Sleepers
1914. Oil. 35½ x 47
Mr. E. N. Seltzer

Evening Glow
1915-1925. Oil on board. 12 x 16
North Carolina Museum of Art

21

Indian Summer
1915-20. Oil. 10½ x 13½
Miss Patricia Carnell

A Wet Day
1890-1900. Watercolor. 8 x 12
Mrs. Arthur E. Howlett and
Mrs. Worth B. Plyler

Mountaineer
1894. Watercolor. 8¾ x 9
Mrs. Arthur E. Howlett and
Mrs. Worth B. Plyler

24

The landscape "Moonlight" (Plate 17) which dates between 1915-1920 reinforces the idea that many of Daingerfield's landscapes embody the religiousity found in his more obviously religious paintings. The three trees portray the artist's trinity, his three selves, and the circular movement of the light encircling the pine trees establishes a halo. [The repetition of the three trees is visible in other works as "Apple Blossoms" (Plate 18).] Further, the mauves, with their spiritually cleansing power, and the greens, with their healing quality, appear a great deal in this painting. The stillness and solemnity of the scene enlarge the religious feeling as does the inner glow of the light in the middle ground. One might criticize an interpretation of this kind; however, it reveals the innermost convictions of the artist. Daingerfield interested himself in the psychic and in Algernon Blackwood. Such an interpretation would not be out of keeping for Blackwood who wrote a story entitled "The Man Whom the Trees Loved" in which a man communicates with the spirits of trees. Daingerfield does a similar thing when he endows the three trees in "Moonlight" with his own spirit.

When Daingerfield first viewed the Grand Canyon in 1911 he saw "the beautiful" in a spectacular and full blown form. He spotted the same colors he had known and painted in North Carolina, but the Colorado sun intensified them and made them more luminous. Years earlier Blind Jenny had prophesized that this large red hole, the Grand Canyon, would be an important place for Daingerfield. Now he was ready to be inspired by the changing reflections of the light on the Canyon's walls and the glorious colors.

The Santa Fe Railway commissioned him to paint scenes of the West as an incentive to railway customers.[30] The paintings were to be large views displaying the beauties found in traveling through the West.

A year after he first sighted the Canyon, Daingerfield produced a painting entitled "The Grand Canyon" (Color Plate on Cover) which he described as his "chief work."[31] One is amazed to perceive that the canvas follows not a literal transcript of any scene but a marvelous recreation of the glowing color and wild grandeur of the place. The entire painting sings out with gorgeous color—opal mountains and crimson peaks are touched with mists of pearl and pink, and the chasms between them vibrate with many colored shadows. Successive layers of glazing build up the coloristic view. And this use of color and paint becomes even more powerful in this painting than in the earlier works. Daingerfield spreads the paint on the canvas in broad masses and leaves the texture of the pigment rather rough in order to break up the surface. The roughness of one layer of paint constitutes a surface on which successive layers of color are super-imposed in

[30]In this exhibition two of the Grand Canyon paintings which Elliott Daingerfield did for the Santa Fe Railway are included. The Divine Abyss" (1911) and "The Lifting Veil" (1913) still remain in the collection of the Santa Fe Railway.

[31]Letter to Mr. Burton Mansfield, the first owner of The "Grand Canyon" from Daingerfield, March 1912.

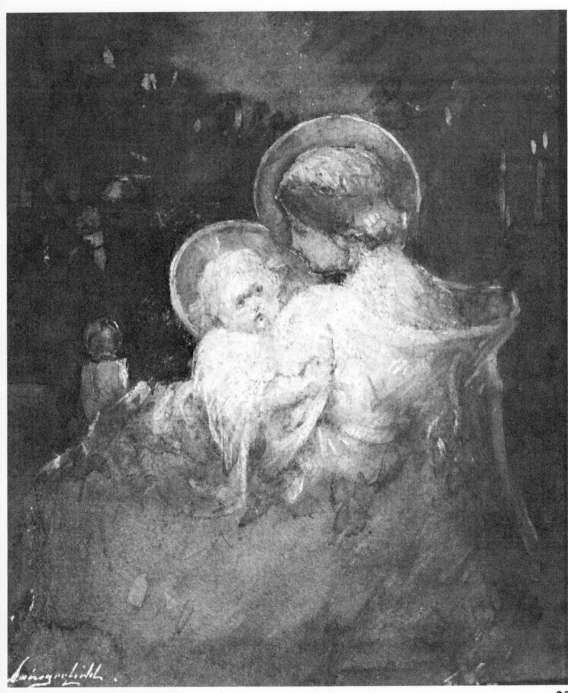

Study for "The Fiske Madonna"
1894-95. Watercolor. 6½ x 5½
Mrs. Arthur E. Howlett and
Mrs. Worth B. Plyler

25

much the same way as the teeth of a comb catch strands of hair. The effect of one through another, the increased luster of tone upon tone, and the magic carrying power of certain colors for certain others hints at innumerable shades of feeling that one could not have conceived with a more direct approach. Starting with the masses of the sky, the rocks and the trees, Daingerfield seems to work all over the canvas as he applies one glaze over another so that each color remains distinct yet varies in mood with those colors closest to it.

Daingerfield painted the majority of the Grand Canyon scenes between 1911 and 1915. Some of them have the quality of "The Grand Canyon" while others grow more intimate with figures symbolizing the spirit of the Canyon. "The Genius of the Canyon" (Plate 19), painted in 1913, displays a large nude as an allegorical manifestation of the timeless quality of the Canyon while a domed city rests on the opposite side of the canvas. Daingerfield wrote a poem which aptly explains the allegory:

> Strip from the earth her crust
> And see revealed the carven glory of the inner world.
> Templed—domed—silent:—
> The while the Genius of the Canyon broods.
> Nor counts the Ages of Mankind
> A thought amid the everlasting calm.

A contemporary description in the "New York Evening Post" says of "The Genius of the Canyon":

> If it were in a railroad station, crowds would miss their trains. Poets have written to it. Its sweetness, its grandiloquence, its coloring (for it has coloring, not color) make it the very ideal for those who do not see a painting, but feel it through the haze of sentimentality.[32]

A year after "The Genius of the Canyon" Daingerfield set forth another allegorical painting, "The Sleepers" (Plate 20) which discloses a different facet of the Canyon's personality. In this oil, sleeping figures nestle in the rocks. A poem was composed by the artist to interpret this allegory:

> Age on age the Sleepers rise
> To see in dreams the canyons splendor rise
> Height from river bed to golden crest
> Gods are they—as you and I,—
> Who see in spirit what the eyes deny.

Daingerfield's last works from 1915 until his death in 1932 reinterpret the coloristic effects of the canyon pictures in a more subtle vein. Mainly, he paints intimate landscapes which show the influence of George Inness' later pictures. With their mystical mood and soft veils of color, these works belong essentially to American Decorative Impressionism. Unlike Inness,

[32] *The New York Evening Post*, 7 April 1917.

Silvery Landscape
1900-20. Watercolor and gouache
8 x 11
Mrs. Arthur E. Howlett and
Mrs. Worth B. Plyler

Daingerfield has a tendency to sprinkle rich greens, blues, or ochres all over the canvas. The paint handled in this manner does not imply objective reality; it merely acts as an emotive device.

In the painting "Evening Glow" (Plate 21) Daingerfield stresses the atmospheric quality which becomes rather heavy and airless. The artist envelops the entire canvas in a type of subjective poetry which is intensified by the spongy softness of the pigment. By applying color in thick and thin veils with one layer of color overlying another, Daingerfield builds up a changing surface quality. These thick and thin waves of pigment seem to be applied with an indolent gesture which helps to impart to the canvas a hazy, dreamlike quality.

He painted "Indian Summer" (Plate 22) in a similar style. Again, one finds the veils of pigment and successive layers of color. Ochre is applied to certain areas of the canvas, and it affects the green of the grass in a different way from the oranges of the trees. Because of the great amount of glazing, the outlines lose their rigidity, becoming more fluid and the forms less architectural. The entire composition flows together. One senses that the lack of definite outlines attempts to arouse in the beholder the feeling of the infinity of the representation. The object always flickers and changes before the spectator's eyes, and this change, this constant flux, becomes the reality rather than the object itself.

Daingerfield continued to paint landscapes similar to "Evening Glow" and "Indian Summer" for the remainder of his life. During a trip to Europe in 1924, however, he became enamoured with scenes of Venice. Perhaps, it was the strain of this trip which caused his physical breakdown in 1925. After the tour Daingerfield never completely recovered, and his lack of strength must be accounted as the reason for the diminishing power of his last works.

He died in 1932 after he had traveled from North Carolina to New York City.

Elliott Daingerfield defies classification. Attempts to label him fall wide the mark. At times he varies from being an "American Millet" to having affinities with the Pre-Raphaelites. Adjectives as Western, Ryderesque, or American Decorative Impressionist apply to only certain periods of his painting and do not encompass the total Daingerfield. His contemporaries referred to him as a tonalistic, or colorist ,or called him an intimate painter. But even labels such as these do not describe the complete man.[33] Perhaps Blind Jenny's prophecy comes closest to defining Daingerfield's importance as an American artist when she decreed to Anna Grainger, "You will marry an artist who will become famous for painting two places. One will be a huge rock in the South and the other a big red hole in the West."

[33]Daingerfield, *Ralph Albert Blakelock*, p. 9. In writing about Blakelock Daingerfield states the following which is applicable to himself also:

There are those who argue that a man may follow a leader with great sincerity. The answer is, in art each man must be a leader, not a follower, for no two are alike, no two souls are given the same message, and while it may amuse the critic to trace likeness, the great truth remains that true art is personal.

Altar Boy Attending St. Peter:
Study for "The Magnificat"
The Lady Chapel of The Church of
St. Mary the Virgin, New York City.
1902-06. Pencil. 19 15/16 x 16
Mrs. Arthur E. Howlett and
Mrs. Worth B. Plyler   27

Uriel: Nude Study for
"The Magnificat" in The Lady Chapel
of The Church of St. Mary The
Virgin. New York City.
1902-06. Pencil. 15 15/16 x 19 15/16
Mrs. Arthur E. Howlett and
Mrs. Worth B. Plyler

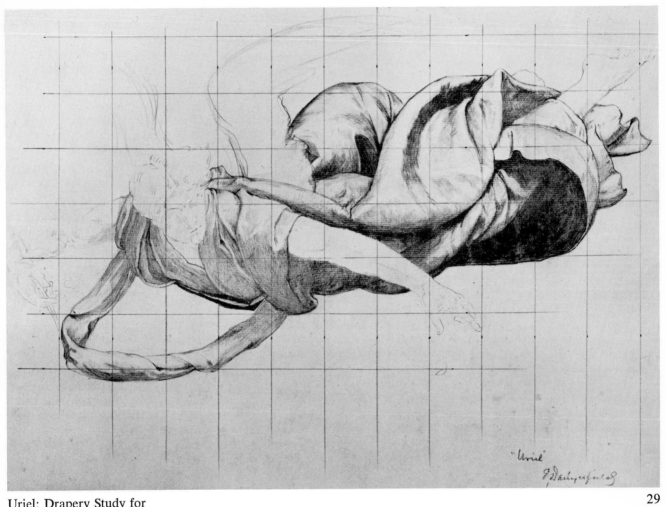

Uriel: Drapery Study for
"The Magnificat" in The Lady Chapel
of the Church of St. Mary
The Virgin, New York City.
1902-06. Pencil. 15 15/ x 19 15/16

Catalogue

The arrangement is chronological, including all mediums. The dimensions are in inches, height preceding width. Unless otherwise indicated all works are paintings in oil on canvas. All water-colors and drawings on paper.

1 **Monk Smelling A Bottle of Wine.** 1880. Signed. 20 x 13. Lent by Mrs. Worth B. Plyler.

2 **Caricature of the Artist.** 1883. Etching. Signed in plate. 11¾ x 7¾. Lent by Mrs. William Thorpe.

3 **Landscape With Trees.** 1884-91. Watercolor. 11 x 9. Lent by Mr. & Mrs. Robert H. Crawford, Jr.

4 **Old Man In The Snow.** 1884-91. Watercolor. Signed. 9 x 12¾. Lent by Mr. & Mrs. Robert H. Crawford, Jr.

5 **The Japanese Corner.** 1885. Signed. 20 x 14. Lent anonymously through the courtesy of Hirschl & Adler Galleries, New York.

6 **Woman Polishing Brass.** 1886. Signed. 20½ x 14½. Lent by Dr. & Mrs. Anderson Page Harris.

7 **Figure With Sheep.** 1887. Signed. 24 x 44. Lent by Don Hartzog, Jr. MD.

8 **Blowing Rock.** 1890. Signed. 13½ x 20. Lent by Mr. & Mrs. Leon Stacks.

9 **Study of Blouse & Skirt.** 1890-1900. Pencil. 15 15/16 x 12½. Lent by Mrs. Arthur E. Howlett and Mrs. Worth B. Plyler.

10 **Seated Figure.** 1890-1900. Pencil. 19⅝ x 15¾. Lent by Mrs. Arthur E. Howlett & Mrs. Worth B. Plyler.

11 **Capri.** 1890-1910. Signed. 24 x 28. Lent by Mr. & Mrs. Joseph D. Dulaney.

12 **Cabbage Patch.** 1890-1900. Signed. 13½ x 19. Lent by Dr. & Mrs. Forrest B. Long.

13 **A Wet Day.** 1890-1900. Watercolor. Signed. 8 x 12. Lent by Mrs. Arthur E. Howlett & Mrs. Worth B. Plyler.

14 **Apple Blossoms.** 1890-1910. 15½ x 19½. Lent by Miss Mandy Richardson.

15 **Swirling Mists.** 1890-1910. Watercolor. Signed. 9½ x 13¾. Lent by The City Art Museum, St. Louis.

16 **Christ Walking On The Water.** 1890-1910. Watercolor. Signed. 19½ x 25. Lent by Mr. Charles A. Cannon.

17 **Study for "The Call of The Winds".** 1911-15. Pencil. 16 x 20. Lent by Mrs. Arthur E. Howlett and Mrs. Worth Plyler.

18 **Flight Into Egypt.** 1890-1910. 20 x 24. Lent by Mr. & Mrs. Joseph D. Dulaney.

19 **Waters of Oblivion.** 1890-1910. Signed. 12⅛ x 8¾. Lent by Dr. Frederick L. Whiting.

20 **Figures In Landscape.** 1890-1910. Signed. 48 x 36. Lent by Mr. Alex E. Mass.

21 **Christ and Nicodemus.** 1890-1910. Signed. 14 x 18½. Lent by Dr. Frederick L. Whiting.

22 **Moon Shadows.** 1892. Signed. 20 x 16. Lent by Mrs. Worth B. Plyler.

23 **The Harvest.** 1892. Signed. 19½ x 15½. Lent by Mr. E. N. Seltzer.

24 **The Pumpkin Girl.** 1892. Watercolor. Signed. 16 x 24. Lent by Mrs. John A. Tate.

25 **The Ewe.** 1892. Signed. 15½ x 19½. Lent by Dr. & Mrs. Forrest B. Long.

26 **Dahlias.** 1892. Signed. 24 x 24. Lent by Mrs. Worth B. Plyler.

27 **Study for "Christ In The Garden of Gethsemane".** 1894. Watercolor. **Sketch of A Woman.** 1894. Pencil. 6 11/16 x 4⅞. Lent by Mrs. Arthur E. Howlett & Mrs. Worth B. Plyler.

28 **Christ In The Garden of Gethsemane.** 1894. Watercolor. Signed. 10¾ x 7½. Lent by Mrs. Arthur E. Howlett & Mrs. Worth B. Plyler.

29 **Mountaineer.** 1894. Watercolor. Signed. 8¾ x 9. Lent by Mrs. Arthur E. Howlett & Mrs. Worth B. Plyler.

30 **Christ At The Garden.** 1894. Signed. 21½ x 39½. Lent by Mr. Charles A. Cannon.

31 **Study for "The Fiske Madonna".** 1894-95. Watercolor. Signed. 6½ x 5½. Lent by Mrs. Arthur E. Howlett & Mrs. Worth B. Plyler.

32 **Still Life With Oranges.** c. 1895. Signed. 16¼ x 22¼. Lent by Mr. Claude B. Williams.

33 **Mysterious Night.** 1895. Watercolor. Signed. 25 x 20. Lent by Mrs. Arthur E. Howlett & Mrs. Worth B. Plyler.

34 **Visit of The Magi.** 1895. Watercolor. Signed. 21 x 29. Lent by Mrs. Arthur E. Howlett & Mrs. Worth B. Plyler.

35 **Will Ye Not Watch With Me One Hour?** c. 1897. Signed. 23 x 32½. Lent by Mr. & Mrs. Joseph D. Dulaney.

36 **Self-Portrait of The Artist.** Before 1900. Mixed Media. 19½ x 14 11/16. Lent by Mrs. Arthur E. Howlett & Mrs. Worth B. Plyler.

37 **As The Sheep Pass By.** Before 1900. Watercolor. Signed. 22¼ x 17. Lent by Mr. Charles A. Cannon.

38 **Drawing of Waterpump and Landscape.** Before 1900. Charcoal on grey paper. 13⅝ x 9 11/16. Lent by Mrs. Arthur E. Howlett & Mrs. Worth B. Plyler.

39 **Study of Trees.** Before 1900. Charcoal. 12⅞ x 9¾. Lent by Mrs. Arthur E. Howlett & Mrs. Worth B. Plyler.

40 **Sketch of Cows and Chickens.** Before 1900. Charcoal. 9 9/16 x 13⅞. Lent by Mrs. Arthur E. Howlett & Mrs. Worth B. Plyler.

41 **Study of The Artist's Daughter, Marjorie, for "The Story of The Madonna".** c. 1900. Pencil. 12 x 16. Lent by Mrs. Arthur E. Howlett & Mrs. Worth B. Plyler.

42 **The Story of The Madonna.** c. 1900. 44½ x 34½. Lent by Mr. Charles A. Cannon.

43 **Drapery Study for "Our Lady of The Rhododendrons".** 1900. Pencil. 16 x 11 15/16. Lent by Mrs. Arthur E. Howlett & Mrs. Worth B. Plyler.

44 **Study of Arm & Hand With Pearls for "Our Lady of the Rhododendrons".** 1900. Pencil. 16 x 17 13/16. Lent by Mrs. Arthur E. Howlett & Mrs. Worth B. Plyler.

45 **Study of Arm and Hand.** 1900. Pencil. 14 x 10 11/16. Lent by Mrs. Arthur E. Howlett & Mrs. Worth B. Plyler.

46 **Study of The Christ Child from the "Holy Family Tondo".** 1900. Pencil. 16 x 11⅞. Lent by Mrs. Arthur E. Howlett & Mrs. Worth B. Plyler.

47 **Holy Family Tondo.** 1900. Signed. 52 in diameter. Lent by Mrs. Arthur E. Howlett.

48 **Garden at Windwood.** After 1900. Watercolor. 11½ x 8⅝. Lent by Mrs. Arthur E. Howlett & Mrs. Worth B. Plyler.

49 **Moon Rising Above Fog Clouds.** Afer 1900. Watercolor. Signed. 7⅝ x 9⅞. Lent by The Metropolitan Museum of Art, New York City.

50 **Landscape With Green Mountain.** After 1900. Watercolor. 10⅞ x 13½. Lent by Mrs. Arthur E. Howlett & Mrs. Worth B. Plyler.

51 **Portrait of Ben Fosdick.** 1900-1905. Charcoal. on blue paper. 23 1/16 x 17½. Lent by Mrs. Arthur E. Howlett & Mrs. Worth B. Plyler.

The following works are preliminary studies for "The Epiphany" in The Lady Chapel of St. Mary The Virgin in New York City:

52 **Charity: Nude Study.** 1902-05. Pencil. 12 x 19. Lent by Mrs. Arthur E. Howlett & Mrs. Worth B. Plyler.

53 **Charity: Drapery Study.** 1902-05. Pencil. 16 x 20. Lent by Mrs. Arthur E. Howlett & Mrs. Worth B. Plyler.

54 **Gaspar: Nude Study.** 1902-05. Pencil. 16 11/16 x 14 9/16. Lent by Mrs. Arthur E. Howlett & Mrs. Worth B. Plyler.

55 **Christ Child: Study of Head.** 1902-05. Pencil. 6¾ x 9⅛. Lent by Mrs. Arthur E. Howlett & Mrs. Worth B. Plyler.

56 **The Virgin Mary: Study of Head.** 1902-05. Charcoal on grey paper. 23½ x 17 15/16. Lent by Mrs. Arthur E. Howlett & Mrs. Worth B. Plyler.

57 **Balthazar: Drapery Study:** 1902-05. Pencil. 12 15/16 x 11 9/16. Lent by Mrs. Arthur E. Howlett & Mrs. Worth B. Plyler.

58 **Gaspar: Drapery Study.** 1902-05. Pencil. 19 13/16 x 15 1/16. Lent by Mrs. Arthur E. Howlett & Mrs. Worth B. Plyler.

59 **Hope: Drapery Study.** 1902-05. Pencil. 14⅛ x 17⅝. Lent by Mrs. Arthur E. Howlett & Mrs. Worth B. Plyler.

60 **Prophet: Drapery Study.** 1902-05. Pencil. 17 5/16 x 15 13/16. Lent by Mrs. Arthur E. Howlett & Mrs. Worth B. Plyler

61 **Melchior: Nude Study.** 1902-05. Pencil. 17 3/16 x 11 13/16. Lent by Mrs. Arthur E. Howlett & Mrs. Worth B. Plyler.

62 **Cherubs.** 1902-05. Pencil. 19⅞ x 15⅞. Lent by Mrs. Authur E. Howlett & Mrs. Worth B. Plyler.

63 **Urn.** 1902-05. Pencil. 12⅞ x 9⅞. Lent by Mrs. Arthur E. Howlett & Mrs. Worth B. Plyler.

64 **Figure of a Man: Drapery Study.** 1902-05. Pencil. 18¼ x 15¾. Lent by Mrs. Arthur E. Howlett & Mrs. Worth B. Plyler.

65 **Cherub With Hammer.** 1902-05. Pencil. 10 15/16 x 11 11/16. Lent by Mrs. Arthur E. Howlett & Mrs. Worth B. Plyler.

66 **Cherub.** 1902-05. Pencil. 15 13/16 x 15 15/16. Lent by Mrs. Arthur E. Howlett & Mrs. Worth B. Plyler.

67 **Soldier: Drapery Study.** 1902-05. Pencil & Charcoal. 15⅜ x 19⅜. Lent by Mrs. Arthur E. Howlett & Mrs. Worth B. Plyler.

68 **Faith: Nude Study.** 1902-05. Pencil. 18½ x 11 15/16. Lent by Mrs. Arthur E. Howlett & Mrs. Worth B. Plyler.

69 **Faith: Drapery Study.** 1902-05. Pencil. 20 x 15 15/16. Lent by Mrs. Arthur E. Howlett & Mrs. Worth B. Plyler.

70 **Seated Soldier: Nude Study.** 1902-05. Pencil. 13½ x 17. Lent by Mrs. Arthur E. Howlett & Mrs. Worth B. Plyler.

71 **Purification: Nude Study.** 1902-05. Pencil. 18⅞ x 11¾. Lent by Mrs. Arthur E. Howlett & Mrs. Worth B. Plyler.

72 **St. Anne: Drapery Study.** 1902-05. Pencil. 19⅞ x 13 9/16. Lent by Mrs. Arthur E. Howlett & Mrs. Worth B. Plyler.

73 **St. Joseph: Drapery Study.** c. 1903. Pencil & charcoal. Signed. 24 x 14½. Lent by Mr. & Mrs. Leon Stacks.

74 **St. Joseph: Study of Head.** c. 1903. Pencil & charcoal. Initialed. 24 x 19. Lent by Mr. & Leon Stacks.

The following works are preliminary studies for "The Magnificat" in The Lady Chapel of St. Mary the Virgin in New York City.

75 **The Virgin Mary.** 1902-06. Pencil. 19⅝ x 14 11/16. Lent by Mrs. Arthur E. Howlett & Mrs. Worth B. Plyler.

76 **Archangel Michael: Nude Study "A".** 1902-06. Pencil. 19⅜ x 11 3/16. Lent by Mrs. Arthur E. Howlett & Mrs. Worth B. Plyler.

77 **Archangel Michael: Nude Study "B".** 1902-06. Pencil. 19⅜ x 11 3/16. Lent by Mrs. Arthur E. Howlett & Mrs. Worth B. Plyler.

78 **Archangel Michael: Nude Study "C".** 1902-06. Pencil. 19⅜ x 11 3/16. Lent by Mrs. Arthur E. Howlet & Mrs. Worth B. Plyler.

79 **Archangel Michael: Armour and Drapery Study.** 1902-06. Pencil. 19⅞ x 15 13/16. Lent by Mrs. Arthur E. Howlett & Mrs. Worth B. Plyler.

80 **Archangel Gabriel: Nude Study.** 1902-06. Pencil. 19⅝ x 14 11/16. Lent by Mrs. Arthur E. Howlett & Mrs. Worth B. Plyler.

81 **Archangel Gabriel: Drapery Study.** 1902-06. Pencil. 19 13/16 x 15¾. Lent by Mrs. Arthur E. Howlett & Mrs. Worth B. Plyler.

82 **St. Stephen: Nude Study.** 1902-06. Pencil. 20 x 13¾. Lent by Mrs. Arthur E. Howlett & Mrs. Worth B. Plyler.

83 **St. Stephen: Drapery Study.** 1902-06. Pencil. 19⅞ x 11. Lent by Mrs. Arthur E. Howlett & Mrs. Worth B. Plyler.

84 **St. Cecilia: Study of Head.** 1902-06. Pencil. 19½ x 15⅜. Lent by Mrs. Arthur E. Howlett & Mrs. Worth B. Plyler.

85 **St. Cecelia: Drapery Study.** 1902-06. Pencil. 19½ x 15⅜. Lent by Mrs. Arthur E. Howlett & Mrs. Worth B. Plyler.

86 **St. Paul: Nude Study.** 1902-06. Pencil. 19 11/16 x 15½. Lent by Mrs. Arthur E. Howlett & Mrs. Worth B. Plyler.

87 **St. Paul: Drapery Study.** 1902-06. Pencil & watercolor. 19 11/16 x 15½. Lent by Mrs. Arthur E. Howlett & Mrs. Worth B. Plyler.

88 **Uriel: Nude Study.** 1902-06. Pencil. 15 15/16 x 19 15/16. Lent by Mrs. Arthur E. Howlett & Mrs. Worth B. Plyler.

89 **Uriel: Drapery Study.** 1902-06. Pencil. 15 15/16 x 19 15/16. Lent by Mrs. Arthur E. Howlett & Mrs. Worth B. Plyler.

90 **St. Ambrose: Drapery Study.** 1902-06. Pencil, charcoal & watercolor. 20 x 15⅛. Lent by Mrs. Arthur E. Howlett & Mrs. Worth B. Plyler.

91 **St. John The Evangelist: Drapery Study.** 1902-06. Pencil. 19⅝ x 15¼. Lent by Mrs. Arthur E. Howlett & Mrs. Worth B. Plyler.

92 **St. George: Nude Study.** 1902-06. Pencil. 20 x 12 13/16. Lent by Mrs. Arthur E. Howlett & Mrs. Worth B. Plyler.

93 **St. Catherine.** 1902-06. Pencil. 14⅛ x 17⅝. Lent by Mrs. Arthur E. Howlett & Mrs. Worth B. Plyler.

94 **St. Elizabeth: Drapery Study.** 1902-06. Pencil. 20 x 12 9/16. Lent by Mrs. Arthur E. Howlett & Mrs. Worth B. Plyler.

95 **Altar Boy Attending St. Peter.** 1902-06. Pencil. 19 15/16 x 16. Lent by Mrs. Arthur E. Howlett & Mrs. Worth B. Plyler.

96 **Celestial Figure: Drapery Study.** 1902-06. Pencil. 20 x 16. Lent by Mrs. Arthur E. Howlett & Mrs. Worth B. Plyler.

97 **Celestial Figure: Drapery Study.** 1902-06. Pencil. 20 x 16. Lent by Mrs. Arthur E. Howlett & Mrs. Worth B. Plyler.

98 **Banner.** 1902-06. Pencil. 19⅞ x 14⅝. Lent by Mrs. Arthur E. Howlett & Mrs. Worth B. Plyler.

The following works are preliminary studies for untitled murals on the other walls of The Lady Chapel of St. Mary The Virgin in New York City.

99 **Saint: Study of Head for Lady Chapel of St. Mary The Virgin.** 1902-07. Charcoal. 23½ x 18½. Lent by Mr. J. C. Crowell.

100 **Saint: Study of Head for Lady Chapel of St. Mary The Virgin.** 1902-07. Charcoal. 23⅞ x 18 5/16. Lent by Mrs. Arthur E. Howlett and Mrs. Worth B. Plyler.

101 **Priest: Nude Study for Lady Chapel of St. Mary The Virgin.** 1902-07. 19 15/16 x 15 1/16. Lent by Mrs. Arthur E. Howlett & Mrs. Worth B. Plyler.

102 **Priest: Drapery Study for Lady Chapel of St. Mary The Virgin.** 1902-07. Pencil (with watercolor). 19⅞ x 13 11/16. Lent by Mrs. Arthur E. Howlett & Mrs. Worth B. Plyler.

103 **Priest: Drapery Study for Lady Chapel of St. Mary The Virgin.** 1902-07. Pencil. 19⅝ x 15¼. Lent by Mrs. Arthur E. Howlett & Mrs. Worth B. Plyler.

104 **Sketch of Seated Woman for Lady Chapel of St. Mary The Virgin.** 1902-07. 19 13/16 x 14 5/16. Lent by Mrs. Arthur E. Howlett & Mrs. Worth B. Plyler.

105 **Blowing Rock Landscape.** 1900-10. Oil on cardboard. 8 x 5⅞. Lent by Mr. & Mrs. William G. Rand.

106 **Study of Madonna and Child (Portrait of Helen McCarthy).** 1900-10. Charcoal on blue paper. 23⅜ x 18¼. Lent by Mrs. Arthur E. Howlett & Mrs. Worth B. Plyler.

107 **Portrait of Helen McCarthy.** 1900-10. Charcoal. 22⅛ x 15 11/16. Lent by Mrs. Arthur E. Howlett & Mrs. Worth B. Plyler.

108 **Portrait of Anna Grainger Daingerfield and Unidentified Figure.** 1900-10. 30 x 36. Lent by Mr. & Mrs. V. Reitzel Snider.

109 **Bathsheba.** 1900-10. Signed. 27 x 19½. Lent by Mr. & Mrs. V. Reitzel Snider.

110 **An Arcadian Huntress.** 1900-10. Signed. 20 x 30. Lent by The City Art Museum, St. Louis.

111 **Grandfather Mountain and Blowing Rock from Windwood.** 1900-10. Oil on cardboard. 7¼ x 9¼. Lent by Mr. & Mrs. William L. Allison, Jr.

112 **Arbor at Windwood, Blowing Rock.** 1900-16. Oil on cardboard. 6½ x 8⅜. Lent by Frank L. Manly.

113 **The City That Never Was.** 1911-14. Oil on cardboard. 9⅝ x 11¾. Lent by Mrs. H. M. Wade.

114 **Sketch of Man, Horse, & Wagon.** Before 1917. Oil on cardboard. 5½ x 7¼. Lent by Mr. & Mrs. Robert L. Lindsey, Jr.

115 **Beech Mountain.** Before 1917. Oil on cardboard. 8 x 10. Lent by Mrs. William L. Allison.

116 **Sketch of Fog In The Mountains.** Before 1917. Oil on cardboard. 8 x 10. Lent by Mr. E. N. Seltzer.

117 **Mountain Landscape.** Before 1917. Oil on cardboard. 7¾ x 9⅝. Lent by Mr. & Mrs. Harry L. Dalton.

118 **Sky Study.** Before 1917. Oil on cardboard. 7½ x 9. Lent by Mr. & Mrs. Harry L. Dalton.

119 **Grandfather Mountain From Yonahlossee Trail.** Before 1917. Oil on cardboard. 7¼ x 9¼. Lent by Mr. & Mrs. Thomas A. Allison.

120 **Stormy Sky.** Before 1917. Oil on cardboard. 5½ x 7½. Lent by Mr. & Mrs. Jack M. Wagner.

121 **In The Garden, Blowing Rock.** Before 1917. Oil on cardboard. 6 x 8. Lent by Dr. & Mrs. T. H. McMillan, Jr.

122 **View of Grandfather Mountain from McRae Meadows.** Before 1917 Oil on cardboard. 5¼ x 7¼. Lent by Mr. & Mrs. William G. Shelton.

123 **Grandfather Mountain from Westglow.** Before 1917. Oil on cardboard. 5¼ x 7¼. Lent by Mr. & Mrs. William G. Shelton.

124 **Birch Trees.** Before 1917. Oil on cardboard. 8½ x 11½. Lent by Mr. & Mrs. John L. Dabbs, III.

125 **Windswept.** Before 1917. Oil on cardboard. 5 x 5¾. Lent by Miss Mandy Richardson.

126 **Summer's Day in North Carolina.** Before 1917. 7½ x 9½. Lent by Mr. E. N. Seltzer.

127 **Forest.** Before 1917. Oil on cardboard. 7¾ x 6. Lent by Mr. & Mrs. Rufus M. Dalton.

128 **Sunset, Blowing Rock.** Before 1917. Oil on cardboard. 5½ x 7½. Lent by Dr. & Mrs. Forrest B. Long.

129 **Showery Day.** Before 1917. Oil on cardboard. 5 x 7¼. Lent by Miss Patricia Carnell.

130 **East from Windwood.** Before 1917. Oil on cardboard. 7¼ x 9. Lent by Miss Patricia Carnell.

131 **Extraordinary Skies.** Before 1917. Oil on cardboard. 5 x 7¼. Lent by Miss Patricia Carnell.

132 **Blowing Rock Village from Windwood.** Before 1917. Oil on cardboard. 6 x 8. Lent by Dr. & Mrs. T. H. McMillan, Jr.

133 **Sketch of Trees in Blowing Rock.** Before 1917. Oil on cardboard. 5⅜ x 7½. Lent by Mr. Charles W. Stanford.

134 **Artists' Studio At Blowing Rock.** Before 1917. Oil on cardboard. 8½ x 10½. Lent by Mr. & Mrs. Alex R. Josephs.

135 **Sketch of Trees.** Before 1917. Oil on cardboard. 8⅛ x 6⅛. Lent by Mr. Frank L. Manly.

136 **Mountain Study.** 1900-17. Oil on cardboard. 5½ x 7¾. Lent by Mr. & Mrs. Alan Dickson.

137 **Grape Arbor—Windwood.** 1900-17. Oil on cardboard. 7¾ x 6. Lent by Mr. & Mrs. Rufus M. Dalton.

138 **Grape Arbor.** 1900-17. Oil on cardboard. 7½ x 9. Lent by Miss Patricia Carnell.

139 **Figures In Landscape.** 1900-17. Oil on cardboard. 6 x 7½. Lent by Mr. & Mrs. Benjamin F. Williams.

140 **Andromeda: Nude Study.** 1900-20. Pencil. 9 13/16 x 10⅜. Lent by Mrs. Arthur E. Howlet & Mrs. Worth B. Plyler.

141 **Silvery Landscape.** 1900-20. Watercolor & gouache. Signed. 8 x 11. Lent by Mrs. Arthur E. Howlet & Mrs. Worth B. Plyler.

142 **"Blowing Rock".** 1900-20. Signed. 24⅞ x 34¾. Lent by The High Museum of Art, Atlanta.

143 **Slumbering Fog.** c. 1905. Signed. 29⅞ x 35⅞. Lent by The Metropolitan Museum of Art, New York City.

144 **Blowing Rock.** 1900-05. Oil on cardboard. 8 x 6. Lent by Mr. & Mrs. William G. Shelton.

145 **Christ Stilling The Tempest.** 1905-10. Signed. 20 x 24. Lent by the Metropolitan Museum of Art., New York City.

146 **Midnight.** c. 1907. Signed. 30 x 36. Lent by The Brooklyn Museum. New York.

147 **Study for "Autumn".** 1900.05. Oil on panel. 6½ x 9½. Lent by Mr. Charles A. Cannon.

148 **Autumn.** 1907. Signed. 30 x 36. Lent by Mrs. Worth B. Plyler.

149 **Sky Study for "High Noon".** 1907-08. Oil on cardboard. 7¾ x 5½. Lent by Mr. & Mrs. David H. Rankin.

150 **High Noon.** c. 1908. Signed. 48 x 36. Lent by Mrs. Arthur E. Howlett & Mrs. Worth B. Plyler.

151 **Study for "Gwennie, Portrait of A Cat".** 1907. Conté crayon. 10 x 6⅞. Lent by Mrs. Arthur E. Howlett & Mrs. Worth B. Plyler.

152 **Gwennie, Portrait of A Cat.** 1908. Signed. 30 x 17½. Lent by Mrs. Worth B. Plyler.

153 **Figure by Reflecting Pool for "Pearls of The Morning".** 1909. Charcoal on blue paper. 15 x 18 15/16. Lent by Mrs. Arthur E. Howlett & Mrs. Worth B. Plyler.

154 **Marjorie in Valentine Costume.** 1910-15. 25 x 18. Lent by Mrs. Arthur E. Howlett.

155 **Sketch of Marjorie Daingerfield.** 1910-15. Pencil. 7½ x 4½. Lent by Miss Mandy Richardson.

156 **Landscape with Hay Figures.** 1910-20. Signed. 28½ x 24. Lent by Maxwell Galleries, Ltd., San Francisco.

157 **Grandfather Mountain #1.** 1910-20. Watercolor. Signed. 9¼ x 12¾. Lent by Mrs. Arthur E. Howlett & Mrs. Worth B. Plyler.

158 **Grandfather Mountain #2.** 1910-20. Watercolor. Signed. 9¼ x 13¼. Lent by Mrs. Arthur E. Howlett & Mrs. Worth B. Plyler.

159 **Moonlight.** 1910-20. 31 x 36. Lent by Hirschl and Adler Galleries, New York City.

160
161 **Sketch for "The Divine Abyss—Grand Canyon"** 1911-13, Oil on cardboard. 9½ x 7½. Lent by Mr. E. N. Seltzer.

The Divine Abyss—Grand Canyon. 1911. Signed. 38 x 24. Lent by Santa Fe Railway, Chicago.

162 **Over The Rim of The Grand Canyon.** 1911-13. Oil on cardboard. 7⅛ x 9⅞. Lent by Mr. & Mrs. Frederick Lewis, Jr.

163 **Sketch of The Grand Canyon.** 1911-13. Oil on cardboard. 7½ x 9½. Lent by Mr. Charles W. Stanford.

164 **Sketch of Sunlight On The Grand Canyon.** 1911-13. Oil on cardboard. 8 x 9⅞. Lent by Mr. & Mrs. Frederick Lewis, Jr.

165 **View of The Canyon.** 1911-13. Oil on cardboard. Signed. 8 x 9⅞. Lent by Mr. & Mrs. Frederick Lewis, Jr.

166 **Hill in Arizona.** 1911-13. Oil on cardboard. 7¾ x 9¾. Lent by Mr. E. N. Seltzer.

167 **Boulders in Arizona.** 1911-13. Oil on cardboard. 7½ x 9½. Lent by Mr. E. N. Seltzer.

168 **Mesa.** 1911-13. Oil on cardboard. 8 x 10. Lent by Mr. & Mrs. William L. Allison, Jr.

169 **The Grand Canyon.** 1912. Signed. 36¼ x 38¼. Lent by The North Carolina Museum of Art, Raleigh.

170 **The Night of the Titanic.** April 14, 1912. Watercolor. 4¾ x 6¾. Lent by Mrs. Worth B. Plyler.

171 **Study for The Genius of the Canyon.** 1913. 12 x 16. Lent by Mrs. Arthur E. Howlett & Mrs. Worth B. Plyler.

172 **The Genius of The Canyon.** 1913. Signed. 35 x 47. Lent by Mrs. Arthur E. Howlett & Mrs. Worth B. Plyler.

173 **The Lifting Veil, Grand Canyon.** 1913. Signed. 32 x 48. Lent by Santa Fe Railway, Chicago.

174 **Opaline Morning, Grand Canyon, Arizona.** 1911-14. Signed. 36 x 48. Lent by Mr. & Mrs. Louis E. McFadden.

175 **Sketch for "The Call of the Winds"**

176 **The Call of the Winds.** 1911-15. Signed. 40 x 32½. Lent by Dr. and Mrs. Francis Robicsek.

177 **The Sleepers.** 1914. Signed. 35½ x 47. Lent by Mr. E. N. Seltzer.

178 **Indian Summer.** 1915-20. Signed. 10½ x 13½. Lent by Miss Patricia Carnell.

179 **Sketch of The Red Sofa Cushion.** 1915-20. Oil on cardboard. 10 x 12. Lent by Mr. E. N. Seltzer

180 **The Red Sofa Cushion.** 1915-20. 27¼ x 33¼. Lent by Mr. & Mrs. Alan Dickson.

181 **Portrait of Marjorie.** 1915-20. Pastel. Signed. 11½ x 14½. Lent by Mrs. Arthur E. Howlett.

182 **Return From The Farm.** 1915-20. Signed. 15 x 20½. Lent by The National Collection of Fine Arts, Smithsonian Institution, Washington, D. C.

183 **Evening Glow.** 1915-25. Oil on board. Signed. 12 x 16. Lent by The North Carolina Museum of Art, Raleigh. Gift of Dr. & Mrs. Aubrey Lee Brooks, Greensboro.

184 **Sunset at Blowing Rock.** 1915-28. Signed. 23½ x 33. Lent by Mr. Charles A. Cannon.

185 **Field and Sky.** 1916-17. Oil on Board. 8½ x 11¾. Lent by the North Carolina Museum of Art, Raleigh. Gift of Mr. & Mrs. William G. Rand & Family in Memory of Major William L. Allison.

186 **Sunset at Westglow.** c. 1917. Oil on masonite. 6¼ x 8¼. Lent by Mr. E. N. Seltzer.

187 **Story Hour.** c. 1918. Signed. 12 x 14. Lent by Maxwell Galleries, Ltd., San Francisco.

188 **Hope and Memory.** c. 1918. Oil on board. Signed. 12 x 10. Lent by Mr. & Mrs. Harold B. VanFossen.

189 **The Sunset Hour.** 1919. 35½ x 47½. Lent by The Butler Institute of American Art, Youngstown, Ohio.

190 **Autumn.** 1920. Signed. 8 9/16 x 11½. Lent by The Mint Museum of Art (gift of Mr. & Mrs. Charles A. Cannon.)

191 **Study for Ben Green's Hill.** c. 1920. Pencil. 5 9/16 x 8 15/16. Lent by Mrs. Arthur E. Howlett & Mrs. Worth B. Plyler.

192 **Ben Green's Hill.** 1920 Signed. 8 9/16 x 11½. Lent by Dr. & Mrs. Charles S. Hobbs.

193 **North Carolina Farm.** 1920-30. Watercolor. Signed. 10½ x 12½. Lent by Mrs. Arthur E. Howlett & Mrs. Worth B. Plyler.

194 **The Golden Hour of Day.** 1922. Signed. 30 x 44½. Lent by Mr. & Mrs. Louis E. McFadden.

195 **Point Lobos, California.** 1923-24. Oil on cardboard. Signed. 8 x 10. Lent by Mr. & Mrs. William G. Rand.

196 **Venetian Scene.** 1924-30. 8 x 12. Lent by Mrs. William L. Allison.

197 **Venetian Scene.** 1924-32. 9 x 12. Lent by Mrs. Arthur E. Howlett.

198 **Venetian Scene.** 1924-32. Oil on cardboard. 9 x 12. Lent by Mr. & Mrs. Joseph D. Dulaney.

199 **Canal, Venice.** 1924-32. Signed. 25½ x 35½. Lent by Mr. Charles A. Cannon.

200 **Venice.** 1925. Oil on cardboard. 9 x 12. Lent by Mrs. Arthur E. Howlett.

201 **View of the Charles Cannon Home in Concord, North Carolina.** 1925-26. Signed. 23½ x 33½. Lent by Mr. Charles A. Cannon.

202 **Sunset Glow.** 1925-28. Signed. 23½ x 33½. Lent by Dr. & Mrs. Forrest B. Long.

203 **Venetian Landscape.** 1927. Signed. 39 x 57. Lent by Mrs. Worth B. Plyler.

204 **Still Life with Flowers.** No date. 33½ x 23½. Lent by Mr. Charles A. Cannon.

205 **Mountain Laurel.** No date. 5¼ x 9¼. Lent by Mr. E. N. Seltzer.

206 **Sunlit Hillside.** No date. Oil on cardboard. 5¾ x 8. Lent by Mr. & Mrs. Harry L. Dalton.

207 **Drapery Study.** No date. Charcoal on grey paper. 23 1/16 x 17½. Lent by Mrs. Arthur E. Howlett & Mrs. Worth B. Plyler.

208 **Angel.** No date. Charcoal. 17 5/16 x 24⅛. Lent by Mrs. Arthur E. Howlett & Mrs. Worth B. Plyler.

209 **Figures.** No date. Pastel. 6⅝ x 9¾. Lent by Mr. & Mrs. Harry L. Dalton.

210 **Landscape with Purple Mountain.** No date. Watercolor. 9 x 10½. Lent by Mrs. Arthur E. Howlett & Mrs. Worth B. Plyler.

211 **Drapery Study.** No date. Pencil. 18 11/16 x 15½. Lent by Mrs. Arthur E. Howlett & Mrs. Worth B. Plyler.

212 **Study of Brocade.** No date. Pencil. 15⅝ x 12 1/16. Lent by Mrs. Arthur E. Howlett & Mrs. Worth B. Plyler.

213 **Nature Study: Landscape with Fence.** No date. Pencil. 9⅞ x 13 11/16. Lent by Mrs. Arthur E. Howlet & Mrs. Worth E. Plyler.

214 **Sketch of Two Trees.** No Date. Pencil. 9⅞ x 6⅞. Lent by Mrs. Arthur E. Howlett & Mrs. Worth B. Plyler.

215 **Study of Branch, Drapery, Hand, and Glove.** No date. Pencil. 15½ x 11½. Lent by Mrs. Arthur E. Howlett & Mrs. Worth B. Plyler.

216 **Crane.** No date. Pencil. 7 13/16 x 4 13/16. Lent by Mrs. Arthur E. Howlett & Mrs. Worth B. Plyler.

217 **Hand Holding Hat.** No date. Pencil. 16 x 11 15/16. Lent by Mrs. Arthur E. Howlett & Mrs. Worth B. Plyler.

218 **Wheat Field.** No date. Signed. 14 x 20. Lent by Mr. Charles Gay.

219 **Crouching Woman: Nude and Drapery Study.** No date. Pencil. 16 x 11⅞. Lent by Mrs. Arthur E. Howlett & Mrs. Worth B. Plyler.

220 **Nude Study.** No date. Pencil. 17⅜ x 13 15/16. Lent by Mrs. Arthur E. Howlett & Mrs. Worth B. Plyler.

221 **The Calf.** No date. Charcoal. 7¾ x 13½. Lent by Miss Patricia Carnell.

Bibliography

Daingerfield, Elliott. **George Inness: The Man and His Art.** New York: Frederick Fairchild Sherman, 1911.

.... "Nature Versus Art," **Scribner's Magazine,** XLIX (February, 1911), 253-56.

.... **Fifty Paintings by George Inness.** New York: Frederick Fairchild Sherman, 1913.

.... **Ralph Albert Blakelock.** New York: Frederick Fairchild Sherman, 1914.

.... **A Collection of Paintings by George Inness.** New York: Henry Reinhardt & Son, 1917.

.... "J. Francis Murphy—Painter," **Scribner's Magazine,** LXI (February, 1917), 127-30.

.... "George Inness," **Century,** XCV (November, 1917), 71.

.... "Color and Form—Their Relationship," **The Art World,** III (December, 1917), 179-80.

.... "Albert Pinkham Ryder, Artist and Dreamer," **Scribner's Magazine,** LXIII (March, 1918), 380-84.

.... "Henry W. Ranger: Painter," **Century,** XCVII (November, 1918), 82-89.

.... "Sketch of the Artist." Unpublished article written between 1925 and 1932 for the University of North Carolina. Manuscript in possession of University of North Carolina Library at Chapel Hill, North Carolina.

.... "Introduction." Inness, George, Jr. **Life, Art and Letters of George Inness.** New York: Century Co., 1917.

Howlett, Marjorie. Hotel des Artistes, New York, New York. Interview, 6 January 1971.

Howlett, Marjorie, and Plyler, Gwendoline. "Westglow," Blowing Rock, North Carolina. Interview taped by Joseph Dulany, 4 September 1967. A copy of this tape is located at the University of North Carolina Library at Chapel Hill.

.... "Westglow," Blowing Rock, North Carolina. Interview, 19 October 1970.

Kasanov, Nina. "American Landscapes of the Nineteenth Century in the North Carolina Museum of Art," **North Carolina Museum of Art Bulletin,** VIII (June, 1969), 3-15.

Kobbe, Gustave. "Mr. Sargent's Latest Pictures." **The New York Herald,** 5 November 1916, p.5.

Louisville Courrier Journal, 19 April 1895.

McMahan, Margaret. "States Most Noted Painter Had Close Ties with City," **Fayetteville Observer,** 10 October 1965, Sec. D. p.1.

Merrick, Lula. "Holbein Studios, First in City Are to Go, But Memories Will Be Bright," **The Sun and New York Herald,** 7 March 1920, p.7.

New York Evening Post, The, 7 April 1917.

Plyler, Gwendoline. Monroe, North Carolina. Interview, 10 February 1971.

Chronology

1859   Born in Harper's Ferry, Virginia, March 26th.
Father: Captain John Elliott Parker Daingerfield.
Mother: Mathilda Wickham De Brua Daingerfield.

1861   Family moved to Fayetteville, North Carolina, where father in charge of Arsenal.

1880   Arrived in New York City on January 12th and entered in a brief apprenticeship with artist, Walter Satterlee. First exhibited in National Academy of Design.

1884   Moved to Holbein Studios where he made the acquaintance of George Inness. Married (September 25th) Roberta Strange French, daughter of Judge Robert Strange French of Wilmington, North Carolina.

1885-86   Stricken with severe attack of diptheria in the winter.

1886   Went to Blowing Rock, North Carolina to recouperate strength after illness, in the summer.

1891   Won "point d'appui" in the Holbein Studios where he closely associated with American artists such as A. H. Wyant, Kenyon Cox and others. Roberta French Daingerfield died in childbirth.

1892   Exhibited "The Mothers" with members of the Salmagundi Club, February.

1894   George Inness died.

1895   Lectured (April 18-19) to the alumnae of Girl's High School in Louisville, Kentucky, "Art It's Expression and Development" and George Inness: "His Life and Work". Married Anna Grainger, daughter of Leander Kaye Grainger of Louisville, Kentucky, December 30th. The Church of St. Mary the Virgin completed in New York City.

1896   Exhibited "Could Ye Not Watch With Me One Hour?" at Lotos Club in New York City, January. Exhibited sketches and studies of the mountains of North Carolina at New York Watercolor Club, November. "Madonna and Child" on cover of Christmas issue of *The Churchman Magazine*. Instructed classes in composition at the Philadelphia School of Design and the Art Student's League in New York City.

1897   Summer Tour of Europe.

1900   Completed "Windwood" his second home in Blowing Rock, North Carolina.

1902   Awarded Clark Prize (for best figure composition) at National Academy of Design for "The Story of the Madonna," May 14th. Elected as associate member of the National Academy of Design. Commissioned to paint murals for the Lady Chapel of the Church of St. Mary the Virgin, New York City.

1902-07   Worked on murals "The Epiphany" and "The Magnificat" for St. Mary the Virgin.

1903 Instructed classes in composition and oil painting from life and still life at Philadelphia School of Design for Women. Elected as a member of Society of American Artists, April 9th. Traveled in Virginia and exhibited "The Story of the Madonna" at Richmond Art Club, May. Elected as active member of Virginia Historical Society, May 12th.

1906 Elected to National Academy of Design.

1907 Exhibited study of "The Figure of the Virgin" for "The Magnificat" at Twenty-second Annual Exhibition of the Architectural League of New York.

1908 Moved from Holbein Studios to Gainsborough Studios on Central Park.

1911 First public exhibition in Boston at R. C. and N. M. Vose Galleries, March. Completed book about George Inness *The Man and His Art*. Viewed Grand Canyon for the first time at the request of the Santa Fe Railroad Company.

1913 Took his family to the West. Stayed in Carmel, California and traveled to the Grand Canyon for the second time.

1914 Exhibited "Trees on the Canyon Rim" at the Cocoran Gallery in Washington, D. C. with the Society of Men Who Paint The Far West, January.
Published *Ralph Albert Blakelock*.

1916 Built third summer home "Westglow" in Blowing Rock, North Carolina. St. Mary's Chapel, Metropolitan Life Insurance Company Sanatorium in Mt. McGregor, New York completed and consecrated, July 25th.

1918 Presented an altar picture, "Madonna of the Hills" to his Church in Blowing Rock, St. Mary of the Hills.

1924 Toured Europe for the second time, began painting Venetian scenes, suffered physical breakdown (an embolism) which arrested his artistic activities, November.

1932 Died in his Gainsborough Studio of a heart attack, October 22nd. Buried in Cross Creek Cemetery in Fayetteville, North Carolina.

1934 Fifty-three of his paintings exhibited in memorial exhibition at Grand Central Galleries, New York City, April 3-21.

1947 North Carolina State Art Society featured Daingerfield in an exhibition, "Daingerfield and His Contemporaries".

Credits

Designed by Steve Galit Associates

Type Composition by Charlotte Composition Company

Printing by Associated Printing Company

The color reproduction on the cover is from a photograph taken by the North Carolina Museum of Art. The remaining photographs are by David Brinning and Assoc., nos. 1, 2, 3, 4, 5, 6, 7, 8, 11, 13, 14, 15, 16, 18, 19, 22; Tom Walters, nos. 12, 20, 23, 24, 25, 26, 27, 28, 29; Metropolitan Museum, nos. 9, 10; Frank Manly, no. 21.